D1454442

Contents

LEARNING RESOURCES CENTRE
Havering College
of Further and Higher education

39111

362.734

Q

1 Introduction

This practice guide updates BAAF's Practice Note 13, *The Placement Needs of Black Children* and Practice Note 26, *The Children Act 1989: The importance of culture, race, religion and language*. It is based on the following premises:

- That placements should meet the individual needs of each child on the range of measures detailed in the Looking After Children (LAC) materials: health, education, identity, family and social relationships, social presentation, emotional and behavioural development and self-care skills; and

- That the legislative requirement to consider racial origin, culture, religion and language applies to every child and every placement.

This practice guide focuses only on family placement needs arising from racial origin, culture, religion and language. However, these needs influence all the others detailed in the LAC materials and must be met alongside them. Needs arising from racial origin, culture, language and religion are likely to require a different emphasis in placement planning and support for majority ethnic,[1] black and other minority ethnic children due to the different experiences of racism and majority or minority status of their group. This does not deny the individuality of each child. Rather, it highlights the importance of recognising needs arising from common experiences related to racism and ethnicity in much the same way as practitioners recognise common needs related to age, experiences of abuse, etc. This guide, therefore, offers *general* guidance in relation to good placement practice in these areas; it does not offer easy answers as these would not serve the complex needs of the individual child. This guide contributes to, but cannot be a substitute for, the professional skill required to make placement decisions that are sensitive to the range of short and long-term needs of each child or sibling group.

Historical background

Britain has always been populated by diverse groups which, from the 16th century, have included groups of black people (Fryer, 1984). The placement needs of black children in Britain were first noted by the Jamaican delegate at the Pan African Congress in 1945 and have remained in focus almost continuously from the mid 1960s. Attention in the 1960s and 1970s focused on increasing the number of foster carers and adoptive parents (primarily white at that time) for black children. The increase in numbers of white parents adopting black children (Home Office Advisory Council on Childcare, 1970) can be attributed to several factors including goodwill on the part of white parents and the decreasing number of healthy white babies available for adoption (from 14,000 in 1968 to 1,400 in 1988).

Attention from the mid 1970s focused on recruiting black parents for black children (ABAFA, 1977). The impetus for this campaign arose from the recognition, primarily by black social workers, of the need for black children to develop a positive black identity and survive racism (Small, 1986). This recognition has succeeded, over time, in increasing the recruitment of black foster carers and adopters, increasing the proportion of black children placed with black carers, and increasing the number of agencies which endorse children's needs for "same race" placements (Waterhouse, 1997). It has influenced the legislation and policy guidelines that now highlight the importance of "race", culture, religion and language in placement and which recommend "same race" placements as the "placement of choice".

The arguments about "same race" placements focus on the "same race" placements of black children only. These are always open to challenge and generate research and policies that attempt to

---

1 In this practice guide majority ethnic or white refers to those belonging to the predominant ethnic group in the UK; minority ethnic refers to those belonging to groups numerically smaller than the predominant ethnic group. Minority ethnic groups are not only those distinguished by their skin colour; they also include others such as Turkish, Jewish and Travelling people or Irish and Scottish people in England. Black refers to those minority ethnic people who are of South Asian, African, African-Caribbean origin and those who are of black and white parentage, commonly referred to as "mixed race". Ethnic group is an imprecise term currently understood as 'people sharing a common culture, language, religion and origin (territorial or ancestral)'.

consider the needs arising from racial origin, culture, religion and language of black children. "Same race" placements for white children continue unchallenged while little research or professional attention is given to considering the needs that may arise from the racial origin, culture, religion and language of white children. Yet both the legislation and the political and professional context suggest that 'due consideration of racial origin, culture, religion and language' should be the right of every child.

2 The legal framework

The United Nations Convention on the Rights of the Child (1989), to which Britain is a signatory, provides a context for domestic law. It states unambiguously that due attention to identity, ethnicity, culture, religion and language in all placement decisions is the right of every child.

> *A child temporarily or permanently deprived of his or her family environment, or in whose best interests cannot be allowed to remain in that environment, shall be entitled to special protection and assistance provided by the State... When considering solutions, due regard shall be paid to the desirability of continuity in a child's upbringing and to the child's ethnic, religious, cultural and linguistic background.*
> (Article 20)

The UN Convention also emphasises this right for ethnic, religious and linguistic minorities:

> *In those states in which ethnic, religious and linguistic minorities or persons of indigenous origin exist, a child belonging to such a minority or who is indigenous shall not be denied the right, in community with other members of his or her group, to enjoy his or her own culture, to profess and practice his or her own religion, or to use his or her own language.*
> (Article 30)

The legislation and guidelines within Britain pertaining to fostering are also unequivocal about the right of every child to due consideration of these factors.

The Children Acts of England and Wales (1989) and Scotland (1995) state:

> *The Local Authority is required to give due consideration...to the child's religious persuasion, racial origin and cultural and linguistic background in arriving at decisions about looked after children.*
> (Children Act 1989 s22 (5c); Children (Scotland) Act 1995 s17 (4(c))

The Guidance to the Children Act 1989 states:

> *It may be taken as a guiding principle of good practice that, other things being equal and in the great majority of cases, placement with a family of similar ethnic origin and religion is most likely to meet a child's needs as fully as possible and to safeguard his or her welfare most effectively.*
> (Volume 3, 2.40)

Guidance to the Children (Scotland) Act 1995 states:

> *When considering the type of placement to be chosen, regard should be paid to a child's racial, religious, cultural and linguistic background. As far as possible, this background should be catered for within the placement, with carers, or one or more staff members, sharing the child's religion and heritage. If possible, the location of the placement should not isolate the child from his or her community or cause him or her to experience prejudice.*
> (Volume 2, p.6, para 26))

The Children (Northern Ireland) Order 1995 states:

> *Before making any decision with respect to a child whom it is looking after, or proposing to look after, a Board shall give due consideration to the child's religious persuasion, racial origin and cultural and linguistic background.*
> (s26 (3)(c))

There is currently less standardisation in the domestic legislation pertaining to adoption. The Adoption (Scotland) Act 1978 endorsed by the Adoption Agencies (Scotland) Regulations 1996, states:

> *In reaching any decision relating to the adoption of a child, a court or adoption agency shall have regard to his religious persuasion, racial origin and cultural and linguistic background.*

The Adoption Act 1976, pertaining to England and Wales, mentions religion only:

> *An adoption agency shall in placing a child for adoption have regard (as far as practicable) to any wishes of a child's*

parents and guardians as to the religious upbringing of the child
(s7)

The UK legislation cited on fostering and adoption, like the UN Convention, is applicable to *all* children. Nevertheless, the government circulars (England and Wales) which have followed this legislation suggest that these sections can be seen as mostly relevant to minority ethnic children, for example, the section on 'Race, Culture, Religion and Language' in LAC 20 (98) on Adoption is subtitled 'Understanding the needs of children from black and minority ethnic communities'. This circular states:

A child's ethnic origin, culture, language and religion are significant factors to be taken into account when adoption agencies are considering the most appropriate placement for a child; however, such consideration has to take into account all the child's needs... Where no family can be identified which matches significantly to the child's ethnic origin and cultural heritage, the adoption agency's efforts to find an alternative suitable family must be pro-active and diligent. The Government has made it clear that it is unacceptable for a child to be denied loving adoptive parents solely on the grounds that the child and adopters do not share the same racial or cultural background (Department of Health, 1998, pp3-4.).

A further government letter, CI (2000) 7 (Social Services Inspectorate, Department of Health, 2000) emphasises the need to be pro-active and diligent in seeking adopters from minority ethnic communities:

Specific recruitment campaigns directed at minority ethnic communities are needed; we have no reason to believe that targeting minority ethnic communities will meet with anything but an encouraging response.
(p.9)

3 The research framework

This practice guide is based on recent British research. While this is less extensive than the North American research, it has the advantages of being specific to this practice context. Much of the recent British research also speaks directly to the young people placed (Thoburn et al, 1998; Ince, 1998; Kirton and Woodger, 1999; Richards and Ince, 2000; Howe and Feast, 2000) thereby avoiding the biases that may be caused by parents responding about the young people's adjustment, ethnic identity and attachment. Their research focus on adolescents and adults enables a fuller picture of identity and adjustment to emerge than with child focused research. Most of these British studies combine qualitative and quantitative data thus furthering our understanding of the complexity of adjustment, attachment and alienation experienced by black children placed in white families. Thoburn et al's research (1998) is particularly helpful in facilitating some understanding of the differences for black children when they are placed with white families compared with those placed with black families. (Much of the North American research omits this dimension and compares minority ethnic children placed in white families to white children placed in white families.) The young people in Kirton and Woodger (1999) and Richards and Ince's research (2000) have been contacted via groups. This may have enabled them to share negative placement experiences while emotionally attached to their adoptive parents and foster carers.

While the limitations in the British research have not been as thoroughly analysed as those of the North American research (Rushton and Minnis, 1997; Kirton, 2000) there are similar limitations including small samples, samples biased by agency and locality, the difficulty of measuring complex concepts such as identity and linked self-esteem, and the failure (with the exception of Howe and Feast, 2000) to include responses from older adults who may be able to reflect on developing identity, self-esteem and adjustment through more of the life cycle. But perhaps the most significant omission from the research data is comparable research on minority ethnic children other than black, and on majority ethnic children.

These limitations have led to this practice guide also being based on knowledge from child development theories, clinical research and the literature and research on anti-racist practice.

4 Continuity in a child's background
Culture, religion and language

The importance of cultural continuity for all children is reflected in the Guidance to the Children Act 1989 (England and Wales): 'a child's need for continuity in life and care should be a constant factor in choice of placement' (Vol. 3, p.33). Promotion of continuity in minority cultural, religious and linguistic traditions reflects a valuing of cultural diversity and a rejection of former assimilationist trends and is explicitly recommended for fostering by the Children Act 1989 and the Children (Scotland) Act 1995 and for adoption by the circular LAC (20) 98:

> Maintaining continuity of the heritage of their birth family in their day to day life is important to most children; it is a means of retaining knowledge of their identity and feeling that although they have left their birth family they have not abandoned important cultural, religious or linguistic values.
> (Department of Health, 1998, p.4)

Placements provide the link with both the past and the future. Some minority ethnic children will enter the "looked after" or adoption system without having had access to the culture, religion or language that is linked to a minority ethnic parent's heritage. Placements that provide the opportunity to experience these, as well as offering the child a rich resource, provide continuity with a collective past and widen options for future ethnic identifications.

Psychological theories (Fonagy et al, 1994) highlight the importance of cultural, religious and linguistic continuity. The evidence of widespread damage inflicted on societies, for example, Aboriginal in Australia, Native American in North America, where placement patterns have ignored cultural, religious and linguistic continuity, reinforce the value of this continuity; so do the testimonies from adults who experienced inappropriate placements in Britain:

> My five children were split up – none in Muslim homes. Eventually they got to go to a mosque once a week. But nothing, nothing about their daily practice.
> (Richards and Ince, 2000, p.66)

> I'm Scottish myself and I come from a different culture. Quite a few foster placements that I had didn't respect that

> I was Scottish.
> (NFCA video, 1994)

Current practice

Richards and Ince's survey (2000) of local authority services for looked after children found that ethnicity, language, culture and religion were reported to be effectively dealt with in 37–62 per cent of foster placement planning and that only 29 per cent of local authorities had mechanisms for ensuring that a child's needs in terms of ethnicity, culture, language and religion were met on a daily basis, with religion being given very low priority. While research demonstrates that white children are overwhelmingly placed with carers of the same racial origin (Cheetham, 1982; Berridge and Cleaver, 1987) black children experience "racially" matched placements to varying degrees (76 per cent of adopted children, Dance, 1997; 47 per cent of adopted children, SSI, 1997; 74 per cent of fostered children, Barn, 1997). This can mask considerable discontinuity in culture, religion and language for many children, particularly refugee children and those from minority ethnic groups other than black.

Culture: practice guidelines

Cultures incorporate ways of being and viewing the world as well as tangible aspects such as dress, music, food, etc. As cultures are neither homogenous nor static all children absorb and reject aspects of the cultures of their home and the world around them and create their own individual blend of cultures. Where possible, placements need to be chosen and supported which can enable all children to value diverse cultures, without stereotyping them, both so that their own cultural range may be enhanced and so that they may avoid the racism based on a negative evaluation of others' cultures.

Children have considerable access to aspects of the dominant culture as this is likely to permeate every family which has been approved by a local authority and pervades the media, schools, peers, etc; continuity of culture for children from majority ethnic cultures is therefore less of an issue for consideration in placement. However, class, regional and individual family differences in culture can be significant factors in continuity/discontinuity and should be considered in placement matching.

It is important that placements are chosen and supported which can provide children from minority cultures with the cultural continuity that they are not able to access in the wider society. As it is the continuity in their day-to-day life that is important (LAC (98) 20, Department of Health, 1998) placement with foster carers/adopters who can provide cultural continuity as a daily experience within the home is to be preferred. As families develop their own cultural blends, there is unlikely to be any exact matching of cultures. Practitioners need to avoid stereotypical and negative views of minority cultures when recruiting families and also seek guidance from the children and their families on the cultural aspects that may be significant to them in their new home.

Where the birth parents of children each have different cultures, placements must be sought which consider the birth parents' wishes, continuity with the child's current cultural patterns, and the need to help the child maintain or gain access in their day-to-day life to those cultures of their birth parents that are most marginalised and therefore least available in the wider society.

Religion: practice guidelines

Matching placements for religion is given additional priority in the Children Act 1989 and the Children (Scotland) Act 1995. For example, the Children Act 1989 Schedule 2 12 (e) and Guidance states that good practice should include the following (Vol.3, p11):

- Placement of children with carers of the religion, if any, of their birth family.[2] It is important that children are placed with carers who can reflect their families' particular observance, for example, Orthodox or Reform Jew, Methodist or Roman Catholic and encourage their religious heritage at a pace and level that meet the individual child's needs.

- Where birth parents are of different faiths, or religious and non-religious, the placement needs to take into account the child's current practice and the wishes of both parents.

Language: practice guidelines

It is essential that all children be placed where they can continue to communicate in their first language. As language can be a significant marker of cultural identity, all children whose cultural identity is marginalised by the wider society will benefit from placements where they can acquire, as well as standard English, languages / patterns of speech / familiarity with some vocabulary which can contribute to their sense of ethnic belonging.

Continuity of culture, language and religion in day-to-day life can best be provided through placements that offer this within the home. This can be complemented by, for example, contact with the birth and extended family, a neighbourhood and friendship network that provide some continuity for the child, or an independent visitor in a fostering placement. However, this can only contribute to filling a "gap"; it cannot substitute for appropriate placement. While the outcomes in terms of continuity of culture, religion and language are influenced by placement, there are other significant influences, including most importantly, the wishes, personality and actual experiences of the individual child.

---

2 The religious requirement may be interpreted slightly differently in Scotland, where the guidelines state that it is the child's religious persuasion that matters rather than the religion of their birth parents.

5 Racial origin

UK legislation instructs that racial origin, as well as culture, language and religion, should be considered when placing children for adoption and fostering. Racial origin encompasses the experience and sense of a racialised identity. These racialised identities (currently predominantly "black" and "white") are the basis for racism (the unequal allocation of resources, life chances and abusive/preferential treatment based on racial categorisation) as well as the basis for collective resistance to racism.

Racial origin is significant in placement because of its link with racism and resistance to racism, its link with identity and self-esteem, and because it is sometimes linked with culture, language and religion. (Ethnic origin is more strongly linked with culture, religion and language.)

Racism permeates all areas of British society in various forms and varying degrees. The Inquiry into the Death of Stephen Lawrence acknowledges finally, without question, the existence of institutional racism[3] in all major institutions in British society. Virdee (1997) suggests that in a 12 month period there will be an estimated 20,000 racial attacks, and 230,000 minority ethnic/black adults will be racially abused or insulted. Racial harassment also permeates the everyday life experiences of children, in schools, in the community and, for black children with a white parent, can also occur within the family (Barter, 1999). Alchtar (1986) found racist name-calling and bullying commonplace in primary schools and wrote of 'a quiet erosion of identity and self-esteem, brought about by nice white children on nice brown children'. While research indicates that black adults and children most commonly experience racial harassment, it can also be experienced by other minority ethnic groups such as Irish, Jewish and refugee adults and children (Garrett, 2000; Smith, 2000; Fratter and Ndagire, 2000).

The significance of racism for placement decisions regarding minority ethnic children has been recognised in government circulars:

> *Racism can take many forms and is a destructive force, especially in the life of a child. Children from minority ethnic groups are particularly vulnerable to racism and its effects. The issue of racism will inevitably arise at some stage in the life of a child at school, work and leisure; the adoptive family will need to prepare the child for when it occurs and how to deal with it so that the child can maintain a positive attitude about heritage. This is true for all children from minority ethnic communities and therefore the responsibility to prepare children to deal with racism rests with all families caring for them. These families may need help in understanding and preparing their children for times when they and their children encounter racism.*
> (LAC (98) 20, Department of Health, 1998, p.4)

This practice guide suggests that minority ethnic children, particularly those from groups which are targets of racism, need to be placed where they can be protected from as well as prepared for racism (a form of abuse) and majority ethnic children need to be placed where they can learn not to participate in racism. Racism is damaging to all children including those who perpetuate it and those who witness it who may learn that bullying, harassment and violence are acceptable.

Current practice

Appropriate placement of children requires that professionals are aware of racism, committed to anti-racist practice and able to assess and support carers who are also aware and committed. Richards and Ince's research (2000) found that one-fifth of agencies responding saw no need for compulsory training in anti-oppressive practice and that the consequences of

---

3 Institutional racism is defined as 'the collective failure of an organisation to provide an appropriate service to people because of their colour, culture or ethnic origin. It can be seen or detected in processes, attitudes, and behaviour which amount to discrimination through unwitting prejudice, ignorance, thoughtlessness and racist stereotyping which disadvantage ethnic groups' (MacPherson, 1999).

limited and unsatisfactory training were recognised by black workers, voluntary groups and service users:

> *I think that they should take into account when training social workers that there is that little bit more black kids will come across. For example, racism in schools, teachers, other pupils, sometimes even in your own family.*
> (p. 25)

While the training programmes for foster carers (NFCA and NVQ) all include material on racism, a recent SSI letter revealed limited training on racism for adopters (Social Services Inspectorate, Department of Health, 2000). Research on placements has provided mixed evidence of whether black children are being placed in appropriate environments vis-à-vis racism. (Unfortunately there is little information about this on white children in placement.) Kirton and Woodger (1999) highlight from their sample of "transracially" placed adoptees that:

> *Most described quite extensive experiences of racial abuse as children giving way to more institutional racism in adult life. Several had had experiences of racism in the extended family and some regarded their adoptive parents as racist, albeit rarely in very overt ways.*
> (p. 74)

Thoburn *et al*, however, state that 'most parents, white and black, described a range of strategies for overcoming the challenge of racism', with black parents being able to draw on their own experience (1998, p.15). The following practice guidelines are offered to facilitate appropriate placements for all children vis-à-vis racism.

Racism: practice guidelines

The following environments should be explicitly sought in the selection of, and facilitated in the training and support of foster carers and adoptive parents:

- Environments where children are/can be protected from being the targets of racism, particularly in their homes and immediate environment; any racism they nevertheless receive being identified as a collective rather than individual problem, openly acknowledged and suitably responded to by their carers, teachers and others.

- Environments where children are/can be helped to recognise that they are not alone in experiencing racism and/or challenging racism and know that those they are attached to have also experienced, survived and/or challenged racism.

- Environments where children can learn not to perpetuate or collude with racism.

Adoption Now: Messages from Research (Department of Health, 1999) recommends placement 'with people who are themselves likely to have experienced negative discrimination...[for] a child whose race or ethnicity is likely to expose them to racism' (p. 115). This may be insufficient to provide the environment outlined above without a parental commitment to anti-racism and the protection of a like community (Wilson, 1987). The diversity and subtlety of racism and Wilson's (1987) finding that politically aware black parents may have an additional advantage in non-verbally demonstrating and role-modelling to black children ways of surviving racism suggest that similar ethnic origin and experiences of racism between parent and child will also be helpful to the child. While these are particularly important for permanent placements they are also relevant to short-term placements. Many short-term placements become permanent placements and even short-term placements should protect children from abusive experiences such as racism.

While there has been little empirical research on the placement environment that encourages all children not to perpetrate or collude with racism, Barter (1999) suggests that the neighbourhood culture is very significant while Derman Sparks (1989) identifies a parental commitment to challenging all bias, including racism, as most likely to be helpful. Practitioners need to pro-actively seek and support these placement environments where all children can learn not to perpetrate or collude with any form of abuse, including racism.

6 Identity and self-esteem

Identity and self-esteem are not mentioned in UK legislation but have underpinned the concern with 'racial origin, culture, language and religion'. They are, however, an explicit part of the assessment framework for all children as demonstrated by the LAC materials (Department of Health, 1995), the Working Together to Safeguard Children document (Department of Health *et al*, 1999) and the Framework for Assessing Children in Need (Department of Health *et al*, 2000). The Utting report (1997) states:

> *A positive sense of identity, of being somebody, of belonging to oneself, is an inner strength which provides the strongest personal defence against harm. Helping children achieve that identity ... ought to be the explicit objective of any organisation entrusted with the care of children. This sense of identity is derived from membership of family and other groups with similar values with which early life experience is shared. Detachment from family and culture plainly impairs its development; membership of a distinctive or disadvantaged community may compound the difficulties; in the case of black children, their situation is further aggravated by the pervasive effects of racism.*
> (p.113)

Identity is now widely accepted as incorporating numerous aspects of self, for example, age, gender, ethnicity, neighbourhood, interests, skills, religion, culture, etc. Self-esteem is also complex and likely to be derived from both internal and external judgements on all these aspects of self. While all aspects of identity and self-esteem are important to the child, the remit of this practice guide enables only one aspect to be fully explored, that related to ethnicity/"race". The meaning of any aspect of racial/ethnic identity for the individual child, the way he/she demonstrates this, the balance of positive, negative and ambivalent feelings towards racial/ethnic identity, will vary between children, and over time for each child. Children may also regard different aspects of this identity i.e. colour, culture, language, religion as primary at different times. Nevertheless, the most appropriate environment is that which positively and continuously facilitates the child owning and feeling comfortable with all aspects of themselves.

Evidence of the importance of a sense of connectedness or genealogical continuity to the identity of all children derives from child development theories (Erickson, 1968; Owusu-Bempah and Howitt, 1997), theories on adoption (Kirk, 1964; Brodzinsky and Schechter, 1990), clinical evidence (Maximé, 1993) and the findings of research into the outcomes for adopted children (Howe and Feast, 2000).

Unfortunately, little research has been undertaken on the conditions that nurture ethnic/"racial" identity and related self-esteem of white children in ways that do not encourage oppressive attitudes and actions (Barter, 1999).

The importance of positive messages on "race", culture, language and religion for black children has been identified by the research of Thoburn *et al* (1998) and Richards and Ince (2000). Most of the research findings suggest that the identity and self-esteem related to ethnicity/"race" of black children are negatively affected by placement with white carers (Gill and Jackson, 1983; Kirton and Woodger, 1999; Howe and Feast, 2000) and positively affected by placement with black carers (Thoburn *et al*, 1998). Other researchers, for example Bagley (1993), have come to positive conclusions on the ethnic identity and linked self-esteem of minority ethnic children (mostly black children) placed with white carers. Some of the data, however, do not fully substantiate Bagley's conclusion (1993) as seen in the finding quoted below:

> *These adopted children* [at age 6–8 years] *often tended to identify themselves as white ... the black and mixed race adoptees* [at adolescence] *move in a predominantly white milieu.*
> (pp. 244, 247)

Adoption Now: Messages from Research (Department of Health, 1999) concludes that:

> *The grounds for matching black with black may lie ... most notably in the nurturing of a black identity and in defence against racism.*
> (p.44)

"Same race", matched placements for white children may therefore be less crucial (Flynn, 2000).

Current practice

There is little evidence as to whether the ethnic identity and linked self-esteem of majority ethnic children are currently being met in placement although Howe and Feast's research (2000) suggests that their overall identity and self-esteem needs can be negatively affected by the adoption process. The evidence from Garrett (2000) and Smith (2000) suggests that the identity and self-esteem needs of minority ethnic groups other than black – in this case Irish and Jewish – are also not being adequately met in placement. Evidence that the ethnic identity and linked self-esteem needs of black children are being met in placement is mixed. Thoburn *et al*'s study of permanent placements suggests that 88 per cent of black children had their ethnic identity needs met and 78 per cent their linked self-esteem needs (1998, p. 21) and that this is facilitated by, but not conditional on, placement with a family of similar racial origin. Kirton and Woodger (1999), Howe and Feast (2000) and Richards and Ince (2000) provide examples of adoption and foster placements with white parents/carers where the needs relating to ethnic identity and self-esteem of black children were not addressed:

I am not sure that there are any strengths [in the care system]*, the identity is a weakness because you don't know where you are going or where you belong.* (Richards and Ince, 2000, p. 56)

Identity and self-esteem: practice guidelines

Aspects of placement which may be helpful in fostering the development of identity and self-esteem, and which may be most necessary for minority ethnic children, include:

- Carers who can acknowledge and continuously, in natural and uncontrived ways, give positive messages to the child about all aspects of their identity, including ethnicity/"race", culture, religion and language;

- Placements where there is a continuity of experiences with the child's and birth family's previous background in terms of ethnicity, culture, language and religion;

- Placements where the child experiences a positive role modelling of significant aspects of their identity including ethnicity/"race";

- Placements in which the above are readily available in neighbourhoods, schools and places of worship.

7 The context of other placement needs

Meeting placement needs on continuity of culture, language and religion, racial origin, racial/ethnic identity and self-esteem in the context of other needs

All children have a range of needs that must be met in placement, as indicated by the LAC materials. The Race Relations Act 1976 places a clear duty on local authorities (including Social Services) to promote equality of opportunity (s71, a,b) which should include black and other minority ethnic children having as equal an opportunity as white children of having all their needs met.

However, evidence of large numbers of black children (including those with a white parent) awaiting adoptive placements and evidence that some of their needs (attachment, social, educational) can be met by white carers (Gill and Jackson, 1983; Bagley, 1993; Quinton *et al*, 1998; Thoburn *et al*, 1998) can be used to attach less significance to the needs that are the subject of this practice guide. That evidence can also support the placement of black children with white carers. Majority ethnic children are not likely to be required to jeopardise their ethnic needs in order to have their other needs met.

Practitioners need to recognise:

• The existence of equal opportunity issues;

• The possibility of alienation from and attachment to ethnically dissimilar families existing simultaneously (Kirton and Woodger, 1999; Richards and Ince, 2000):
  My foster parents are white and I love them very much and I would die for them, but increasingly as you get older you realise how alienated you are.
  (Richards and Ince, 2000, p. 56)

• The value of being attached to a family with whom you can feel a sense of identification and connectedness;

• The possibility of reasonable self-esteem about some aspects of identity, for example, emotional security or educational attainment existing simultaneously with low self-esteem around racial/ethnic origin;

• The benefits of integrating into a sense of self, racial/ethnic identity and related self-esteem;

• The value of a positive black (or other minority ethnic) identity – and continuity of culture, language and religion – and its role in buffering racism;
  - The extremely negative consequences for some children when the above is not made available (Maximé, 1986);
  - The resilience of many others in meeting complex and often painful challenges when the above is not made available (Kirton and Woodger, 1999).

Adoption Now: Messages from Research (Department of Health, 1999) concludes:
> *The fact that black or mixed-parentage children had become attached to their white adoptive parents is not in itself a conclusive argument for departing from the policy that children should be found ethnically compatible families with respect to new placements; nor is the fact that, judged against the particular outcome criteria and time scales that were applied, no significant difference was detectable between cross-cultural and convergent placements. There are other questions – identity, vulnerability to racism and the lifetime implications once people have left the adopted home – to be considered as well.*
> (p. 116)

Delay

Concern about delay may result in the placement of black children in white families where they are less likely to have all their needs met. LAC (98) 20 states:
> *The Government has made it clear that it is unacceptable for a child to be denied loving adoptive parents solely on the grounds that the child and adopters do not share the same racial or cultural background.*
> (Department of Health, 1998)

The concern that delay impacts on attachment is based on theories of child development (Bowlby, 1969) which are applicable to all children. While much research evidence supports the importance of early placement (Thoburn *et al*, 1998) this is not uniformly substantiated by other studies of fostering and adoption placements (Bagley, 1993; Berridge and Cleaver, 1987; Quinton *et al*, 1998). *Adoption Now: Messages from Research* (Department of Health, 1999) states both that:

> ... *the younger the child the less likelihood of a poor outcome* [and] *one message that stands out above all others is that there is no single factor that leads to success or to instability in a placement, but the way in which several factors combine and interact.*
> (p. 15)

Therefore, while it would seem inappropriate to jeopardise any child's long-term needs based on identity, self-esteem, continuity of culture, language and religion by inappropriate and rushed placements, it also seems in the interest of all children that appropriate placements are made with minimum delay.

Current practice

The SSI letter C1 (2000) 7 identified that:

> *For some children the wait for adoptive families may be a long one with one-third of the children waiting for more than a year.*
> (Social Services Inspectorate, Department of Health, 2000, p.8)

Reasons identified included the lack of a social worker, lack of social work time for adoption, lack of planning, lack of information systems, lack of responsibility by senior management, and failure to recruit adequate numbers of minority ethnic families (Social Services Inspectorate, Department of Health, 2000). *Adoption Now: Messages from Research* (Department of Health, 1999) attributes some of the delay to procedures linked to parental opposition and to information gathering and suggests both that some of the delay could be avoided with better understanding and clarity and that:

> *It should not be assumed that everything should be accelerated. From the child's*

> *point of view and from the adopters things may move too fast.*
> (p.124)

Richards and Ince (2000) highlight from their research into minority ethnic looked after children in their national survey of local authorities that, while there were some excellent initiatives, inappropriate placements were due to a lack of policies, planning, competent recording, awareness, training and commitment, a lack of support for black staff, weak links with black voluntary organisations and failure to implement ongoing recruitment and support of minority ethnic carers. They found that only 38 per cent of local authorities had a specific recruitment policy for black and other minority ethnic carers. However, Barn's research in three authorities (1997) found greater efforts and greater success at recruiting black carers.

Meeting all needs with minimum delay: practice guidelines

While the ability to meet all needs with minimum delay is dependent on agency resources and policies, practitioners need to do the following.

- Seek placements which meet all the needs of every child including those arising from culture, language, religion, and racial origin utilising every available resource, for example, minority ethnic community groups and inter-agency placements.

- Consult with the child, family and with specialist workers as to the priorities appropriate to the individual child or sibling group if all needs cannot be met within a timescale appropriate to the individual child, while remembering that whether or not deemed a priority in a particular case, "race" and heritage are integral to all needs.

- Ensure that unmet need in any area is recorded and senior management notified so that pro-active initiatives in recruitment, training and support can be undertaken by the agency.

- Ensure that resources are put in place that can contribute to meeting unmet need in any area and their outcomes monitored.

8 Matching where there are diverse ethnicities

The complex genealogical and personal histories of many children requiring placement (white and black) determine that "matching" remains a sensitive exercise requiring significant knowledge and expertise. It is essential that some practitioners in each agency develop these rather than the agency placing hurriedly or inappropriately. In placing children with complex ethnic backgrounds, the following considerations should be paramount in meeting ethnic needs:

- Meeting the wishes of the child and parent and continuing positive aspects of a child's life, for example, cultural perspectives and a sense of belonging, whilst ensuring that racism and marginalisation within a birth family (if it has occurred) is not replicated within a substitute family.

- Ensuring that the child is well placed to positively develop those heritages that are most minimised or devalued in wider society, such as being black, Muslim, Irish, Jewish and thus better equipped to cope with the disadvantage and discrimination they are likely to meet throughout life.

- Ensuring that the valuing and reflection of these heritages does not diminish the promotion of, or access to, other identities of the child.

Access to dominant identities and heritages, such as white, English, heterosexual, Anglican, non-disabled is less likely to be an issue. For example, a child of Polish and English parentage is likely to retain access to his/her English heritage if placed with a Polish family. Similarly, a black child with a white parent is likely to retain easy access to white role models and the public aspects of their white heritage, if placed within a black family (Prevatt-Goldstein, 1999). A white sibling, placed with his/her black sibling, in a black family, is also likely to retain access to white role models and the public aspects of their white heritage.[4] Nevertheless, each child needs to be placed in a family where he or she can feel that *all* aspects of themselves are valued.

---

4 Mullender (1999) explores placement of sibling groups including black and white sibling groups. See also forthcoming BAAF practice guide on sibling placements, *Together or Apart?*

9 Agency guidelines

Guidelines for agencies to enable them to provide placements which can meet all the needs of all children, with minimum delay, can be found in CI (2000) 7 (Social Services Inspectorate, Department of Health, 2000) for adoption and the *National Standards for Fostering* (NFCA, 1999). Guidelines that focus on the needs of minority ethnic children are summarised in Richards and Ince (2000 p. 6, p.80). Some of the recommendations most pertinent to the good practice highlighted throughout this practice guide now follow.

The first requirement is for a pro-active, diligent and rolling recruitment programme for foster carers and adopters. This must be based on an audit of children in need and children looked after in the local authority. Attention must be paid to recruiting a range of carers and adoptive parents who can provide a continuity of culture, language and religion for majority ethnic and minority ethnic children. This requires a recognition of the cultural and religious diversities within the local communities. Barn (1997) and Richards and Ince (2000) suggest that recruitment of families able to care for children of black and white parentage, children of minority ethnic groups other than black and for sibling groups, older children and disabled children from a range of cultural and religious backgrounds is urgently needed.

Targeted and rolling recruitment requires robust recording systems for religion, language, culture and racial origin of children, their parents, foster carers and adoptive parents and monitoring systems that are sensitive to children inappropriately placed or waiting for permanent placements. All systems require workers committed to and competent at maintaining them.

Successful recruitment requires workers with adequate time, skills, commitment and agency support. Research suggests that black workers may be particularly successful in recruiting black families but often receive inadequate agency support (Richards and Ince, 2000).

Successful recruitment of majority ethnic and minority ethnic carers and adoptive parents requires working in partnership with existing carers, adoptive parents and community groups. Richards and Ince's research (2000) suggests that much greater efforts are needed to achieve this with minority ethnic carers and community groups.

Successful recruitment needs to be followed by efficient and thorough systems for assessing, preparing and supporting adoptive parents and foster carers. These also require workers from majority and minority ethnic groups who are skilled at assessment and committed to anti-racist and culturally appropriate practice and who are supported by rolling training programmes and an agency culture committed to maintaining this awareness and skill. Agencies also need to commit adequate resources to monitor these processes and to adequately maintain them. Comprehensive post-adoption support and allowances are essential in the recruitment and retention of a wide range of families.

It is essential that adequate resources are allocated to working with the child, including the allocation of a social worker skilled at direct work with children and committed to anti-racist and culturally appropriate practice, and to planning with the child and their family for appropriate placements within agreed timescales. This may include rehabilitation with immediate or wider family, non-related foster care or that with relatives or friends, adoption, or periods of residential care.

Matching of children to short-term placements requires as thorough a consideration of all their needs including those arising from racial origin, culture, language and religion as long-term placements. Inadequate placements (short- and long-term) must be the exception, authorised by senior management, and accompanied by comprehensive and long-term "packages" arranged to contribute to meeting any unmet needs. The value of inter-agency placements that may meet these needs must be carefully considered alongside their appropriateness for contact.

In order to achieve the guidelines above it is essential that the appropriate and speedy placement of all children is owned by senior members of social services.

10 Placement of black children: specific guidelines

Black and minority ethnic children (including those with one white parent) have been considered within this practice guide. Good practice in the placement of black children will now be highlighted[5] as this issue has generated both controversy and practice dilemmas. These specific guidelines are based on the child development theories and analysis of research evidence outlined earlier and which underpin the general guidelines.

Every child needs a family in which to grow and thrive. For the vast majority of black children, as with all children, the best place for them is within their own family. This underpins the Children Act 1989 and the Children (Scotland) Act 1995. Families may be supported in continuing to care for their children by an adequate network of services and by more specific family support and may be encouraged to re-engage in caring for their children by targeted reunification work (BAAF, 1996).

However, research suggests that black families receive less adequate services, for example, housing, employment (Butt and Mirza, 1996); less family support (Butt and Box, 1998) and their children are received into the "looked after system" more speedily than their white counterparts (Barn, 1997). Two groups which may be particularly at risk of receiving inadequate or inappropriate services are refugee children and families and families of single white mothers with black children. Much greater efforts are required to ensure black families have access to appropriate services, support systems and preventative social work intervention.

The Children Acts of both England and Wales and Scotland have highlighted the appropriateness of seeking placements with relatives. Greater efforts are required to seek and support, financially and otherwise, relative and friend carers (BAAF, 1996). This involves changes in resource allocation and in the ethos of social work practice. Placement with relatives and friends, while enabling attachment and security, must also facilitate positive identity and continuity of heritage. Nevertheless, some children will require time limited or permanent substitute placements with families not known to them. For a black child this placement should be with a black family that reflects his/her ethnicity.

Placement with a black family

A black family is more likely to provide a black child of the same ethnic background with the following:

- Positive black attachment figures which the child can internalise;

- An environment where the black child is normal rather than exceptional;

- A range of black role models coping with everyday life;

- A resource for ways of coping with and challenging racism.

A family of similar culture, religion, language and class to the child being placed is additionally likely to provide:

- Continuity with some aspects of the child's heritage;

- Access to aspects of culture, not available in the dominant society, which involve ways of being and ways of seeing as well as ways of doing;

- Access to some of the symbols which enable the child to fit comfortably, if they so wish, with their ethnic group/class;

- A secure and informed framework in which to reject or adapt aspects of their heritage.

The ability of any particular family to meet a child's needs can never be assumed. There are additional factors which need to be taken into consideration, for example:

- Black families will provide the above to different degrees and in different styles;

- Not all black families will be able to provide the above and the requirement for careful assessment of black families remains, as with white families;

5 These guidelines may also be helpful in placing white children of diverse ethnicities.

- Black families need to nurture positive attachment and security and meet the individual needs of the child, as well as provide the above;

- Black families need to be valued and supported (as foster carers, adoptive parents or in post-adoption support) in maintaining the above.

Placement with a white family

There will be gaps in what most white families can offer a black child, because of dissimilarities in "racial" identity, a lack of shared experience of racism, an inability to provide black primary attachment figures as well as some of the other factors noted above. These gaps may be particularly damaging to children who will already have experienced separation, loss and discontinuity (Prevatt Goldstein, 1997). There can also be a qualitative difference between black perspectives being an integral part of the home environment and approach of the principal carer, and being only occasionally made available to the child (Kirton and Woodger, 1999).

Delay is an important factor and drift in the care system must be avoided for all children. There should be a clear plan for each child and individual timescales. Social workers, having made intensive attempts to locate a black family, and in consultation with specialist black practitioners, may deem it in the best interests of a particular black child to be placed with a white family. *Adoption Now: Messages from Research* (Department of Health, 1999) advocates that:

> ...*such discretion has to be exercised within a framework of policy about what is normally expected. The question arises as to how far the reasons for failing [to observe these policy injunctions] are analysed and justified.*
> (p.116)

It is essential that such placements remain exceptional, and that the placement decisions are analysed, justified and authorised by senior management.

Kirton and Woodger (1999) and Thoburn *et al* (1998, p.28) indicate that some white families can successfully parent black children. The available research suggests that these white families and their extended families must be able to demonstrate an active understanding of the developing needs of the black child; an understanding of racism; commitment to challenging racism and discrimination; the provision or development of networks which can include those of their own extended family or of their child's birth relatives; and enable the child to have access to cultural frameworks which will provide continuity for the child.

Nevertheless, the task must not be underestimated as some white families may, despite their best efforts, have difficulty in sustaining these throughout their child's childhood into adulthood. Kirton and Woodger (1999, pp. 74-6) and Thoburn *et al* (1998, pp. 34-41) provide detailed guidance on the assessment and support needed for all families engaged in parenting black children. Kirton and Woodger (1999) warn that a one-off training programme is unlikely to engender any fundamental and lasting change in attitude and a careful assessment by aware and competent workers of foster carers' and adoptive parents' current attitudes, with examples, is needed.[6]

---

6 BAAF's Form F (2000) requires an assessment of the family's ability to parent a child from a different ethnicity.

11 Some practice dilemmas

What if the child looks white?

There are no stereotypical ways of looking white or black. The child should learn to be proud of his or her "racial" and cultural heritage. If the child denies a black parent and attempts to "pass for white", this can lead to psychological problems in the child's future. The child needs to be in an environment where he or she can value all aspects of their heritage, especially those aspects that will be under-valued in wider society, as explained earlier. Therefore, placement with a carer who will not collude with a child's denial of black heritage will enable the child to develop the skills he or she will require for healthy future functioning.

But some children actually say they will not go to a black home...

Social workers sometimes say that black adolescents are refusing to live with black people. This is a sad example of the internalisation of the negative messages that society still gives to black children about being black. The majority of white children who are abused or neglected by white parents do not enter public care stating that they do not want to live with another white family, and if they did then there would, quite rightly, be concern about this from the parties involved. The fact that black children are said to express such negative views about black families should be considered as an indictment of the racism prevalent in wider society as well as in public care, and equally viewed with concern. The child/young person must learn that, like the white population, black people are individuals – some are good, some are not.

We do not, however, suggest that such a child should be placed in a black family without proper preparation. This would be setting the child and the family up to fail. However, if the child is placed with a white family at any stage, it is absolutely essential that the family does not collude with the child over the denial of their black heritage. A plan of work needs to be undertaken which can help the young person begin to unlock the negative messages they have internalised about black people, their relatives and ultimately themselves. The plan and intervention will depend on the individual children, their ages and their expectations, as well as, most critically, the commitment and understanding of the workers and carers involved.

It is worth emphasising that the child's wishes and feelings have to be considered in light of his or her age and understanding. It is also essential to take account of the young person's actual experience with regard to the views he or she may express. No child should be given the burden of decision making which has long-term/life-long consequences. This responsibility belongs with adults.

> *I ended up with a white family at nine years old because I specifically requested it. My social worker was fine about it. It made it easier for her ... and it made my life easier ... Today I struggle to reconcile living with a white family. I think my biggest regret is that I wasn't with a black family.*
> (Richards and Ince, 2000, p. 44)

A mother says she does not want her baby to go to a black family...

The social workers must try to find out why the mother is saying this. It could be that she has internalised the attitudes towards black people caused by racism or it could be something much simpler. Parents may have different views about the most important characteristics of a new family and therefore about what would be best for their child and these views must be explored. Sometimes their expectations of the placement and their wishes for the child may be unrealistic and social workers will need to discuss this with them sympathetically. While every consideration needs to be given to children's and parents' views in every placement, the duty of the agency is to find the family that best meets the needs of the baby, through childhood into adulthood (LAC (98)20, S.20).

The child is settled with white foster carers. Surely it will do more harm than good to remove her?

Practitioners need to strenuously avoid placing children in short-term situations which do not meet their needs, be diligent and speedy in seeking appropriate long-term placements, and work with short-term carers and children to enable children to move on and make new attachments. Practitioners need to assess whether the quality of the attachment on the part of the carers is based on the reality of the child as a black child and if it can meet the developing needs of that child into adolescence and through to adulthood. Practitioners need to assess the ability of the carers and their extended family to provide the environment identified in Section 10 (see subsection titled Placement with a white family). Practitioners need to recognise that the child's attachment may need to withstand growing feelings of alienation and difference as the child develops into adulthood and meets institutional as well as personal racism. Decisions need to be based on the individual situation. If the decision is that the child should stay, practitioners need to recognise the possible long-term consequences for the child and ensure that the carer has the social work support and resources to meet the needs of the child as fully as possible. If the decision is to move the child, practitioners need to locate this within the social work task of removing children from environments that do not meet their basic needs, engage with the feelings of loss of both the child and the carers as well as with their own feelings of contributing to disruption and loss while acknowledging the long-term benefits to the child.

The child is of Chinese, white Irish, and African-Caribbean parentage. How long should we wait for the perfect match?

We can reduce waiting times for any child if efforts are sustained in recruiting widely from local and national populations. This is a clear message from the Children Act 1989 (Schedule 2 11 (b)), LAC (98) 20 and C1 (2000) 7. We also need to use wisely any waiting time to prepare the child for placement. With the diversity within cultures and within families there can be no perfect match. Children need to be placed in the best possible environment, using the guidelines suggested in Section 8, *Matching where there are diverse ethnicities*, as soon as appropriate. It requires a skilled professional decision to determine the appropriate time for each child and the best possible environment the child can be placed in, bearing in mind the possible effects of delay on attachment and the long-term consequences of genealogical discontinuity, negative identity and self-esteem.

The black child is disabled. Which need comes first – disability or "race"?

As highlighted in Section 7, *Meeting all needs*, placements must be pro-actively and diligently sought which meet *all* assessed needs. Any prioritising of needs must be made only after a full assessment and on an individual basis. Specific recruitment, encouragement and support are required to secure and retain adequate numbers of carers (white and black) for children with disabilities.

Surely it is more complicated than just about being black. We would not want to place a Muslim Pakistani child with Catholic African-Caribbean carers...

We need to place children with due regard to religion, ethnicity and all their other needs. As stated previously, this requires sound and pro-active recruitment based on an audit of local needs and extensive local and national enquiries. Where appropriate matches can not be secured, there should be a full discussion with families, consultation with black specialist workers, and a professional decision guided by the criteria outlined earlier. It may be that placement with a black Muslim family from the African continent, with networks within the Pakistani community and which can demonstrate both the ability and the commitment to enabling the child to access these, is the most acceptable alternative to the child and family and is the best available match within a time-scale appropriate to the child's needs.

In looking for a family which can actively reflect, value or promote a child's ethnic and cultural heritage, it is necessary to assess which of the families available has the best access to resources that will meet the child's present and long-term needs. For each child, an individual decision must be made bearing in mind that all black families, whatever their ethnicity, share the common experience of racism. Black families are also more likely than most white families to have access to a wide range of cultures through experience of living in multicultural areas within Britain, and for some families, through their experiences in multicultural communities abroad.

Should we place with a black single parent in a white area or a white couple in a multiracial area?

Research by Owen (1999, p.68) has indicated good placement outcomes in agencies which prioritised "racial" matching including placement with black single parents which appeared to be preferable to placing black children with white couples. It is important that the value of single carers is recognised within the framework of careful assessment of the needs of the particular child.

The black children studied in both Owen's (1999) and Thoburn *et al*'s (1998) research have reinforced the importance of children seeing their ethnicity and racial origin reflected in their neighbourhood and schools (Department of Health, 1999, p.44). This should be a factor in the matching for placement of all minority ethnic children. However, families may not draw their networks from their neighbourhood, particularly when the neighbourhood does not reflect their class or ethnicity and families may change neighbourhoods. The neighbourhood is likely to reinforce a positive home environment or partially remedy existing gaps. It cannot substitute for the advantages found within the home.

12 Conclusion

This practice guide has addressed the implications of racial origin, culture, religion and language, identity and self-esteem for *all* children. It has identified that these are both significant for all children and require a different emphasis in placement depending on the degree of racism and marginalisation experienced by the child's ethnic group. It has therefore provided guidelines for the placement of majority ethnic *and* minority ethnic children. This practice guide encompasses both institutional and individual practice and makes recommendations as summarised below.

- Resources (financial, appropriate staffing, social work training, administrative and monitoring procedures) need to be allocated to maintaining children in birth and extended families where possible and in placing children appropriately with relatives and friends.

- Resources need to be allocated to planning for children separated from their birth families, and to undertaking direct work with children to prepare them for reunification, or permanency with substitute families, or appropriate residential care.

- Resources need to be allocated to recruiting, training and supporting majority and minority ethnic carers and adoptive parents to enable appropriate matching with minimum delay.

- Recruitment, training, support and matching must entail proactive attention to securing placements which can nurture identity and self-esteem; promote continuity of culture, religion and language; buffer and challenge racism as well as meet the other needs of the child.

- Time-scales must acknowledge the importance of early secure attachments and the importance of locating placements best able to meet the child's long-term as well as short-term needs.

- Social work managers, workers and carers need to challenge the culture of racism which limits the priority placed on black/minority ethnic children having all their needs met and which makes it difficult to acknowledge the particular strengths black/minority ethnic carers may have in the direct care of children from similar cultures and who are likely to experience similar discrimination.

The policy and practice recommended in this guide are endorsed by the findings of the recent large scale, DoH funded research:

> *The requirement in the Children Act 1989 and the accompanying guidance to seek to place children with parents who can meet their identified needs as individuals, and who are of similar cultural and ethnic background, provides a sound basis for policy ... this would be the view of all but a tiny minority of the parents and children who gave us their opinions on this question, including members of ethnically mixed and ethnically diverse families.*
> (Thoburn *et al*, 1998, p. 27-8).

13 References

ABAFA (1977) *The Soul Kids Campaign*, London: Waterloo Press Ltd.

Alchtar S, 'They call me Blackey', *The Times Educational Supplement*, 19.9.1986.

BAAF (1996) *Planning for Permanence*, Practice Note 33, London: BAAF.

Bagley C (1993) *International and Transracial Adoptions: A mental health perspective*, Aldershot: Avebury.

Barn R, Sinclair R and Ferdinand D (1997) *Acting on Principle: An examination of race and ethnicity in social services provision for children and families*, London: BAAF.

Barter C (1999) *Protecting Children from Racism and Racial Abuse*, London: NSPCC.

Berridge D and Cleaver H (1987) *Foster Home Breakdown*, Oxford: Blackwell.

Bowlby J (1969) *Attachment and Loss – Vol. 1*, Harmondsworth: Penguin.

Brodzinsky D and Schechter M (eds) (1990) *The Psychology of Adoption*, Oxford: Oxford University Press.

Butt J and Box L (1998) *Family Centred: A study of the use of family centres by black families*, London: REU.

Butt J and Mirza K (1996) *Social Care and Black Communities: A review of recent research studies*, London: HMSO.

Cheetham J (1982) (ed) *Social Work and Ethnicity*, London: George, Allen and Unwin.

Dance C (1997) *Focus on Adoption: A snapshot of adoption patterns in England – 1995*, London: BAAF.

Department of Health (1995) *Looking After Children (LAC) Materials*, London: HMSO.

Department of Health (1998) *Adoption: Achieving the right balance*, Local Authority Circular (98) 20, London: HMSO.

Department of Health (1999) *Adoption Now: Messages from research*, London: Wiley.

Department of Health, Department for Education and Employment, Home Office (2000) *Framework for the Assessment of Children in Need and their Families*, London: The Stationery Office.

Department of Health, Home Office, Department for Education and Employment (1999) *Working Together to Safeguard Children*, London: The Stationery Office.

Derman Sparks L and ABC Task Force (1989) *Anti-Bias Curriculum: Tools for empowering young children*, Washington, DC: National Association for the Education of Young Black Children.

Erickson E (1968) *Identity, Youth and Crisis*, London: Faber and Faber.

Flynn R (2000) 'Black carers for white children: shifting the same race debate', in *Adoption and Fostering*, 24:1, pp 47–52.

Fonagy P, Steele M, Higgit H and Target M (1994) 'The theory and practice of resilience', in *Journal of Child Psychology and Psychiatry*, 35:2, pp 23–57.

Fratter J and Ndagire B K (2000) 'Meeting health and ethnic needs in placement: planning for African children affected by HIV', in *Adoption and Fostering*, 24:1, pp 34–9.

Fryer P (1984) *Staying Power*, London: Pluto Press.

Garrett P M (2000) 'Responding to Irish invisibility' in *Adoption and Fostering*, 24 (1) pp 23–33.

Gill O and Jackson B (1983) *Adoption and Race*, London: Batsford.

Home Office Advisory Council on Child Care (1970) *A Guide to Adoption Practice*, London: HMSO.

Howe D and Feast J (2000) *The Long Term Experience of Adopted Adults*, London: The Children's Society.

Ince L (1998) *Making It Alone – A study of the care experiences of young black people*, London: BAAF.

Kirk H (1964) *Shared Fate*, New York: Free Press.

Kirton D (2000) *Ethnicity and Adoption*, Buckingham: Open University Press.

Kirton D and Woodger D (1999) 'Experiences of transracial adoption; assessment, preparation and support: implications from research', in BAAF (ed) *Research Symposium Papers 1998*, London: BAAF.

MacPherson W (1999) *The Stephen Lawrence Inquiry*, London: The Stationery Office.

Maximé J (1993) 'The importance of black identity for the psychological well being of black children', *ACPP Review and Newsletter* 15 (4) pp 173–179.

Mullender A (ed) (1999) *We are Family: Sibling relationships in placement and beyond*, London: BAAF.

National Foster Care Association (1994) *Choosing to Foster* (video), London: NFCA.

National Foster Care Association (1999) *National Standards for Fostering*, London: NFCA.

Owen M (1999) *Novices, Old Hands and Professionals: Adoption by Single People*, London: BAAF.

Owusu-Bempah J and Howitt D (1997) 'Socio-genealogical connectedness, attachment theory and child care practice', *Child and Family Social Work*, 2, pp 199–207.

Prevatt Goldstein B (1997) 'Black children with one white parent – a parent's perspective', in *BAAF Seminar Papers*, London: BAAF, pp 57–64.

Prevatt Goldstein B (1999) 'Black with one white parent: a positive and achievable identity', in *British Journal of Social Work*, 29, pp 285–301.

Quinton D, Rushton A, Dance C and Mayes D (1998) *Joining New Families: A study of adoption and fostering in middle childhood*, London: Wiley.

Richards A and Ince L (2000) *Overcoming the Obstacles, Looked After Children: quality services for black and minority ethnic children and their families*, London: Family Rights Group.

Rushton A and Minnis H (1997) 'Annotation: transracial family placements', *Journal of Child Development and Psychology*, 38:2, pp 157–9.

Small J (1982) 'New black families', in *Adoption and Fostering*, 6:3, pp 35–39.

Small J (1986) 'Transracial placements: conflicts and contradictions', in Ahmed S, Cheetham J and Small J (eds) *Social Work with Black Children and their Families*, London: Batsford.

Smith G (2000) 'Meeting the placement needs of Jewish children' in *Adoption and Fostering*, 24:1, pp 40–7.

Social Services Inspectorate, Department of Health (1997) *For Children's Sake: Pt II An SSI inspection of local authority services*, London: HMSO.

Social Services Inspectorate, Department of Health (2000): *C1 (2000) 7 on LAC (98) 20 – Adoption: Achieving the Right Balance: Response to issues arising from SSI survey of local authority social service departments' implementation of the circular*, London: The Stationery Office.

Thoburn J, Norford L and Rashid S (1998) *Permanent Family Placement for Children of Minority Ethnic Origin*, London: Department of Health.

Utting W (1997) *People Like Us: The report of the review of safeguards for children living away from home*, London: HMSO.

Virdee S (1997) 'Racial harassment', in Modood T and Berthould R (eds), *Ethnic Minorities in Britain: Diversity and disadvantage*, The Fourth National Survey of Ethnic Minorities, London: Policy Studies Institute.

Waterhouse S (1997) *The Organisation of Fostering Services: A study of arrangements for the delivery of fostering services in England*, London: NFCA.

Wilson A (1987) *Mixed Race Children: A study of identity*, London: Allen and Unwin.

Acts

The Children Act 1989 (England and Wales)
The Children (Scotland) Act 1995
The Children (Northern Ireland) Order 1995
The Race Relations Act 1976

HAVERING COLLEGE OF F & H E

39111

BAAF Publications on Black Children ▬

– Order all 3 and save money!

Acting on Principle

An examination of race and ethnicity in social services provision for children and families

Ravinder Barn, Ruth Sinclair, Dionne Ferdinand

Five years on, how had social service departments responded to the duty placed on them by the Children Act 1989 to consider the racial and cultural needs of children in their care? This study explores 196 case histories from three different local authorities and highlights the urgent needs of a growing number of mixed-race children. Important recommendations to both central and local government make this essential reading for all those responsible for the strategic management of services to black and white children and families, and for social workers working with black children.

Commissioned by the Commission for Racial Equality

110 PAGES A4   ISBN 1 873868 40 5   £10.95 + £2.00 p&p   1997

Making it Alone

A study of the care experiences of young black people

Lynda Ince

Based on the personal experiences of ten young black people who had recently left local authority care or a private foster placement – and who had all spent some time in transracial placements, had experienced problems with their racial identity, and felt unprepared for the process of leaving care – this book offers valuable insights into their experiences, feelings and opinions, vividly described in their own words.

'I would recommend it as an informed read for anyone trying to manage or support young black people in the care system... the conclusions could be applied to other minority or perceived minority groups within the care system.'   Jim Clifford, Adoption UK

94 PAGES A4   ISBN 1 873868 51 0   £10.95 + £2.00 p&p   1998

Working with Black Children and Adolescents in Need

Edited by Ravinder Barn

With its emphasis on direct work, this collection offers the reader useful practice-based suggestions for improving strategies and techniques in working with black children and young people in need. Themes tackled include the development of a strong ethnic identity; developing anti-racist and anti-discriminatory practice; communicating with and assessing black children; meeting the needs of transracially adopted black children; meeting educational needs; and preparing care leavers for independence.

'An important book (which) will be very valuable whether you are a worker or manager in the field of social work or related professions ...also useful for educators and students in social work to help further their teaching and learning in anti-oppressive practice.'
Ashok Chand, Child and Family Social Work

176 PAGES A5   ISBN 1 873868 71 5   £12.95 + £2.00 p&p   1999

Order from British Agencies for Adoption and Fostering, Skyline House, 200 Union Street, London SE1 0LX UK. Tel: 020 7593 2072 (Publications Sales), Fax: 020 7593 2001. E-mail: pubs.sales@baaf.org.uk.

Payment by UK sterling cheque (payable to *BAAF Registered Charity*), Access, Visa or Switch credit card or we can send you a pro-forma invoice. Order all three titles and we will supply post-free (SAVE £6.00).

Registered charity number 275689

**B
A
A
F**